WORCESTER
THEN & NOW
IN COLOUR

PAUL HARRISON

First published in 2011

The History Press
The Mill, Brimscombe Port
Stroud, Gloucestershire, GL5 2QG
www.thehistorypress.co.uk

ISBN 978 0 7524 6326 1

Typesetting and origination by The History Press
Printed in India
Manufacturing managed by Jellyfish Print Solutions Ltd

CONTENTS

ACKNOWLEDGEMENTS

My thanks go to:

The History Centre at Worcester Record Office for access to their picture archive; the Dean and Chapter of Worcester for out-of-season access to the cathedral tower; Jane for the midnight elimination of my (too) many commas; Oscar for walking the streets and pathways with me, trying to see my points of view; and to all those unnamed or forgotten, whose enthusiasm and prescience has given us their present: our past.

ABOUT THE AUTHOR

Paul Harrison is fascinated by environments and what people do to them – and nowhere more so than in his home town Worcester. He has pursued many careers throughout his lifetime, working as a photographer, writer, designer, teacher and publisher. He likes good music and quiet cafés.

INTRODUCTION

A book of contrasts such as this will inevitably lead to questions of progress against preservation. Worcester is a beautiful cathedral city with a rich visual legacy but looking at its ghosts can sometimes lead to uncertainties about its present.

It is, perhaps, easy to criticise the town planners of the 1950s, 1960s and 1970s for their lack of foresight in preserving our heritage. Looking back, as we are doing here, at Worcester's old buildings and street patterns, it seems criminal that much of the urban landscape was condemned to oblivion in what seems, from our contemporary perspective, like a very short reign of terror waged on buildings.

The truth, of course, is more complicated and rather less exciting. After the Second World War ideas of a new society and a new vision emerged. The Festival of Britain in 1951 demonstrated new ideas in architecture: modern, straight, clean and uncluttered. By the end of the 1960s, families had attacked the family home, tearing out fireplaces, flush-panelling doors and squaring-off their furniture. There was a mood of modernism, whose basic credo was the rejection of the traditional.

On a municipal level, councils could not approve the cost of the renovation of historic buildings, and what fresh new architect would want to restore the work of others when they could create something individual? Why not risk a little notoriety by making the public sit up and take notice and shock them with the new?

Worcester had its problems. Its growth as an industrial city had put cloth weavers and glove makers into communities living in buildings that had their roots in medieval times. As in other cities, houses accommodated several families, and several houses often shared a courtyard with limited facilities. By the middle of the twentieth century much of Worcester's housing was overcrowded, unsanitary and neglected. The war on squalor had to start. Ironically, as the 1960s youth started to exhibit a nostalgic fondness for the elegance of Victoriana, provincial architecture was locked into its rolling programme of clearance and simplification.

Worcester, however, has retained a higher proportion of historic buildings than most cities, and is more or less at the centre of Britain's biggest concentration of 'black and white' timber-framed houses. Many of the city's medieval buildings survive but it is painful to see the loss of others. In particular, the damage done in the last half of the twentieth century by weighting the planning in favour of cars has done the most to destroy the human-sized walkways and byways that can be seen in the historic photographs. It is also difficult to excuse the clutter of street furniture that now bombards us with advertising and information overload and obstructs some fine views.

Worcester, 'The Faithful City', has remained true to its roots. There are parts where perplexing planning decisions have been made, but if you avoid the concrete and wheelie bins and look above the plate glass shopfronts at the Georgian window lines, you can lose yourself in an earlier age when tightly-knit housing communities with tiny pubs on every corner flourished by the river or around the High Street. You can trace curved routes past wavy-framed wooden houses and courts, and explore the many staging inns where iron-shod wheels clattered towards the stables. If you do not see them yet, you only have to look at the pictures.

Paul Harrison, Worcester, 2011

HIGH STREET, CATHEDRAL END LOOKING NORTH

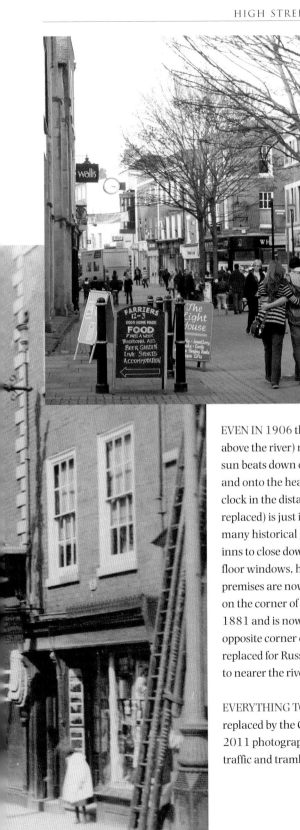

EVEN IN 1906 the High Street (literally, in Worcester's case, above the river) mingled the old and the newer (left). The sun beats down on the shops' protective window awnings and onto the heavily-dressed Worcester shoppers. The large clock in the distance (still there though the building has been replaced) is just in front of the Golden Lion, one of the city's many historical gathering places and the last of the High Street inns to close down. The lion itself, mounted just above the first floor windows, has recently come back after re-gilding, and the premises are now those of Costa Coffee. The curved building on the corner of Pump Street was a more recent addition from 1881 and is now occupied by a jeweller. The building on the opposite corner of Pump Street with the lower roofline was replaced for Russell and Dorrell's furniture store (now removed to nearer the river).

EVERYTHING TO THE right foreground of the picture has been replaced by the Cathedral Plaza shopping centre seen in the 2011 photograph above. The High Street is now vehicle-free: traffic and tramlines have been replaced by trees and people.

HIGH STREET AND LICH STREET

THE OLD PHOTOGRAPH on the left shows the area at the
Cathedral end of the High Street, looking north towards The
Cross. The High Street was a little longer then, extending out
to this curved structure, which echoes that on the corner of
Pump Street (seen in the distance). The road going off downhill
to the right is Lich Street and is remembered with fondness by
many. Like Friar Street, which it met at the bottom of the hill,
Lich Street contained several medieval buildings including the
Old Deanery and the Lich Gate from which, of course, the street
took its name. A lich (or lych) gate is a covered entrance to a
churchyard, in this case St Michael's in College Street, and this,
the last intact cathedral lich gate in the country, was latterly
used as a regular pedestrian passageway between the two streets.

ELGAR'S STATUE NOW surveys a scene in which no trace
remains of Lich Street as neither the gate nor its surroundings
survived beyond the mid 1960s (above). The curved corner of
the High Street junction and the first few buildings behind were
cleared for the dual carriageway and roundabout seen here.
Others gave way to the new shopping centre, formerly named
the Lichgate Centre (later Lychgate) and now Cathedral Plaza.
The Friar Street end of Lich Street ended ignominiously as a
multi-storey car park entrance.

HIGH STREET AND
THE CATHEDRAL

THIS IS THE end of the High Street looking south towards the cathedral in 1910 (right). The presence of the printer and stationer is evidence of the activity of the book, magazine and pamphlet production that had been healthily running in this street since the eighteenth century. Another sign (by the lamp) proclaims 'Ye Olde Glove Shoppe Est'd 1798', which not only supports another famous Worcester product but also proves that nostalgia is not just a recent phenomenon. The large building on the right is still there, currently a building society, but the premises next door went to create Deansway's dual carriageway from what was then Palace Yard outside the Bishop's Palace. The curved-looking building in front of the cathedral lives on today, selling antiques, and the carriage's wheels are at what is now the end of the High Street shopping centre.

THE BUILDINGS ON the left of the street are all gone, giving a wider, clearer view of the cathedral, though this is still somewhat obscured by trees (left). Elgar's statue is positioned not only to look at the place where many of his works have been performed but also as a reminder that his inspiration began in those defunct High Street buildings where his father and uncle had a music shop.

HIGH STREET WIDENING
AT THE CROSS

DURING THE EARLY years of the nineteenth century, tramways came to the High Street, and here we have street improvements to accommodate them. The widening of the High Street near The Cross caused the removal of these buildings to reveal the newer replacement building behind. Demolition here is revealing an old timber-framed structure that has been remodelled and re-faced in keeping with nineteenth-century style. All the visible buildings on the left of the street remain today, and at the time of the old photograph on the left (probably 1904) were recently finished. Broad Street leads off to the right of the photograph and the clock just behind remains today, though in altered form.

THE TRAMS HAVE come and gone, and High Street is wider and brighter, with a view down its entire length (above). The absence of cars and the central line of trees provide the area with a relaxed, open feel; the High Street serves as an antidote to the busy traffic routes that circle the city centre.

THE CROSS

THE CROSS (RIGHT) is the continuation of High
Street going north (away from the cathedral). In
medieval times there was a cross and, presumably,
a market. For cartographers it has been the central
point of Worcester (just as Charing Cross is to
London). The main street flows on beyond The
Cross into The Foregate, then Foregate Street,
then The Tything. The photograph on the right
probably dates from the very early 1900s, and
people linger on the pavement edge, perhaps
waiting to cross or awaiting transport home,
but the young man standing in the road is more

concerned with the spectacle of the camera than the oncoming cab behind him. The cyclist is turning into Broad Street on the left, though he too will have to dodge a man standing in the road preoccupied by some business of his own. A policeman lurks behind him but also seems more interested in the camera than any possible traffic accident. Dick's, the large shop on the left, was one of many shoe stores in the High Street.

TODAY PEOPLE CAN linger safe from traffic to watch street performances, meet friends, eat or just shop (left). The architecture is largely intact, though the street-level shopfronts, being less individual, seem banal by comparison. St Nicholas' domed church on the right is now a tastefully restored restaurant and bar, and the view still stops at the railway bridge next to Foregate Street Station.

THE HOP MARKET AND THE FOREGATE

THE FOREGATE IS home to Worcester's Hop Market. Barclays Bank, along with a fine hotel, was part of this structure, which was built in 1904 to replace the previous Hop Market. The photograph above from the mid to late 1920s displays the fine terracotta arches, bays and mouldings common to the whole building. Despite the damp-looking ground, the sun is on the top of the building, and the chauffeur's boots shine as much as the car.

HOPS ARE NO longer traded in Worcester city centre but the Hop Market exists today as a courtyard of shops with its entrance just to the left of the modern photograph (opposite). Barclays has now moved to the High Street, and their previous premises has been taken by a clothes shop. This area is now a very busy part of the city's one-way traffic system and the idea of one's chauffeur waiting patiently outside seems more in keeping with fiction than finance.

FOREGATE STREET

THIS VIEW (LEFT) down Foregate Street and The Tything was taken somewhere between 1881 when the tramlines were laid and 1894 when the buildings on the right were replaced with the present library and art gallery. A cab and a delivery vehicle trundle northwards and a man leans on a lamp post outside Acacia House. This private accommodation is hidden by the house with the iron balcony and is to be let. It was a three-storeyed, double-bayed Georgian stucco building and showed its non-conformity by being, like the nearby Shire Hall, set back from the street. Further down, the Saracen's Head Hotel offers food and stabling.

ACACIA HOUSE and its neighbours were replaced with something even finer: the Victoria Institute, designed as museum, library, art gallery and art school (above). Simpson and Allen were the designers, and King George V laid the foundation stone in 1894. Two years later it opened to the public. The remainder of the street line has changed very little, and the iron balcony is still present. The Saracen's Head remains as a pub.

THE VICTORIA INSTITUTE

THE VICTORIA INSTITUTE looking south towards the railway bridge. This photograph (left) was taken in 1903, before 'rational dress' freed women from cycling in heavy, voluminous skirts. The Shire Hall to the left, whose railings can be seen, was busy enough to have its own taxi rank with a rest hut for the cabbies.

TODAY THE TYTHING is a busy road, being the main northbound exit channel from the city. The Victoria Institute building looks as impressive as ever, though at least some of its contents may soon be moving to the new riverside university complex, which will provide more expansive public library facilities.

FOREGATE STREET
LOOKING TO THE CROSS

LOOKING TOWARDS THE Cross (left), with St Nicholas' spire right of centre, behind the tower of the Hop Market. The reason for the bunting is unclear as this photograph was taken shortly after 1928. The glass canopy on the right of the picture belongs to the Star Hotel, dating from the sixteenth century and once Worcester's principal staging inn, with coaches departing every day for destinations all over the country.

THE FIRST THREE buildings on the left of the picture no longer exist, as they were demolished for the entrance to Foregate Street Station (see above). A small branch of Tesco, handy for homeward-bound travellers and popular with pupils commuting to the city's schools, now occupies a set-back position here. The Star Hotel has now become the Worcester Whitehouse Hotel and remains one of the city's principal accommodation venues. The cars crossing the road are leaving The Butts and entering Sansome Walk, the road down to Lowesmoor.

SILVER CINEMA/ODEON

THE SILVER CINEMA in 1939 looking north, with the shadow of the railway bridge over
the building next door, can be seen in the old photograph on the left. The cinema occupied a
building created to house the city museum's collection in 1836. Fifty years later, when it had
outgrown its accommodation, the idea of a combined cultural learning centre had grown in the
public mind and the Victoria Institute was the eventual result.

THE SILVER CINEMA and its neighbours are gone now, and the sunlight through the bridge
now shines on a modern, larger Odeon in a very similar position. The cinema, styled to reflect
the art deco cinemas of the mid twentieth century, is one of two mainstream film chains in
Worcester: one at the south of the town centre and this one at the north.

BROAD STREET, TOWARDS THE RIVER

BROAD STREET WAS once a very busy road carrying Worcester's traffic directly to Bridge Street and then over the river. Consequently, it is the main road from The Cross and it developed as a shopping street from early times. Like The Cross and the axis streets of High Street and Foregate Street, it has, in this picture on the left at least, the same elegance of individuality. Skan's tobacconist at No. 69 was a long-established firm who sold a general range of goods for gents and took pride in their window displays; in the nineteenth century George Lewis had a very successful stationery business here during the boom years of letter writing.

THE CURRENT OWNERS have preserved the building well, and the curved glass windows, now displaying Cornish pasties, are intact (above). Unfortunately, the next three buildings have disappeared since the 1950s photograph. One of them, No. 68, next door to Skan's, was the chemist George and Welch, which was formerly Lea and Perrin's. This was the shop where the famous Worcestershire Sauce was invented, developed and marketed before the two partners moved on to their new factory near Shrub Hill Station.

BROAD STREET, TOWARDS THE CROSS

THIS IS BROAD Street (left), looking east to The Cross. Not a very familiar scene now, as many of the buildings have gone, but there are two familiar names: Halfords cycle shop is the building that protrudes towards the centre of the picture – the vertical writing down the white wall spells out the name – and Marks and Spencer have a sign on the third building from the left. The cars and cloche hats suggest that it was taken in the 1920s. Just visible before Halfords is the rounded building that marks the entrance to Angel Place.

BATHED IN SUNLIGHT (above), the entrance to Angel Place still has the same buildings on its corners but looking in the same direction now reveals a mix of old and new, with the Crowngate shopping centre dominating the north side and new street level façades on the right.

BROAD STREET AND ANGEL PLACE

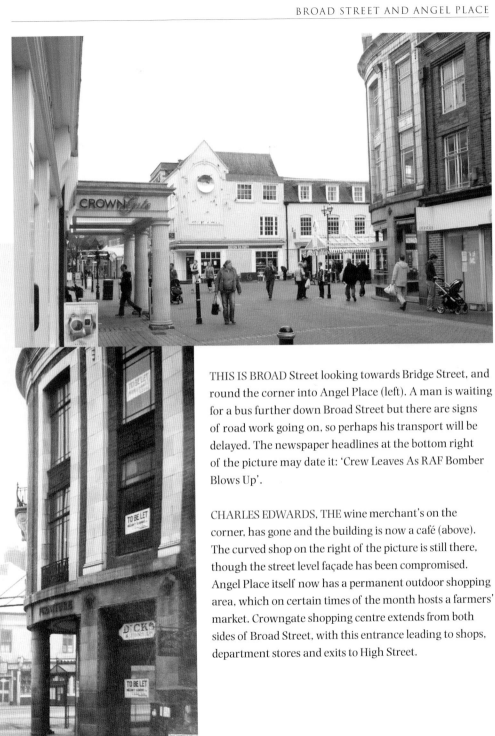

THIS IS BROAD Street looking towards Bridge Street, and round the corner into Angel Place (left). A man is waiting for a bus further down Broad Street but there are signs of road work going on, so perhaps his transport will be delayed. The newspaper headlines at the bottom right of the picture may date it: 'Crew Leaves As RAF Bomber Blows Up'.

CHARLES EDWARDS, THE wine merchant's on the corner, has gone and the building is now a café (above). The curved shop on the right of the picture is still there, though the street level façade has been compromised. Angel Place itself now has a permanent outdoor shopping area, which on certain times of the month hosts a farmers' market. Crowngate shopping centre extends from both sides of Broad Street, with this entrance leading to shops, department stores and exits to High Street.

ANGEL PLACE

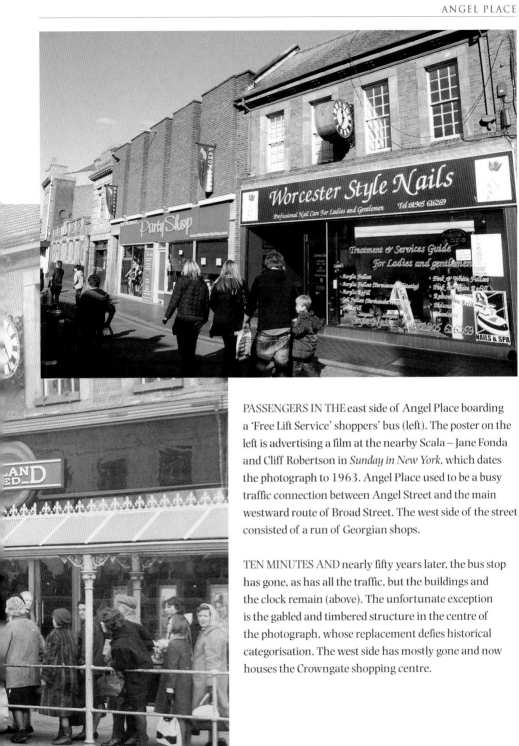

PASSENGERS IN THE east side of Angel Place boarding a 'Free Lift Service' shoppers' bus (left). The poster on the left is advertising a film at the nearby Scala – Jane Fonda and Cliff Robertson in *Sunday in New York*, which dates the photograph to 1963. Angel Place used to be a busy traffic connection between Angel Street and the main westward route of Broad Street. The west side of the street consisted of a run of Georgian shops.

TEN MINUTES AND nearly fifty years later, the bus stop has gone, as has all the traffic, but the buildings and the clock remain (above). The unfortunate exception is the gabled and timbered structure in the centre of the photograph, whose replacement defies historical categorisation. The west side has mostly gone and now houses the Crowngate shopping centre.

ANGEL STREET

THE OLD PHOTOGRAPH on the left shows Angel Street, running from Angel Place to The Foregate, whose buildings can be seen at the end of the street. Dominating the view, the principal building in the street is the Theatre Royal. There had been a theatre here since the eighteenth century and in this view from the early part of the twentieth century it is in good Georgian shape with a curved glass canopy supported by decorative ironwork to protect its queues, and those being delivered and collected by road, from the elements. Because the glasswork overhung the narrow pavement, it was taken down in the 1940s, but by the time the theatre closed in the mid 1950s, a simpler one had appeared. Next door to the theatre, towards The Foregate, is the Shakespeare Hotel, a fortuitously named inn offering pre- and post-theatre refreshments. The other buildings offer a continuation of the Shakespeare's lines, and the street ends in a taller finale to match the structures on The Foregate.

THERE IS LITTLE remaining now: the inn is still there, now a cricket-themed pub; the tobacconist shop survives but without its shop windows; the theatre site holds a cuboid concrete supermarket, which is set back from the line of its neighbours; and the remainder of the buildings have been replaced by a modern brick block currently housing McDonald's.

COPENHAGEN STREET

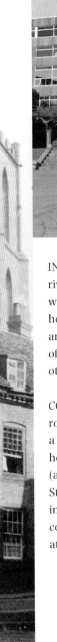

IN 1928 THIS was the view looking up Copenhagen Street from the river (left). Like all the riverside areas, it had housing on both sides with a mixture of terraces and courts. As the population increased, housing became overused and run down. These houses were occupied by artisans, particularly glove makers. St Andrew's Institute at the bottom of the street was a popular social centre. The church towers over the other buildings.

COPENHAGEN STREET IS nowadays a convenient but characterless route between High Street and the river, having at the High Street end a fire station and the rear entrance to the Guildhall. At the bottom, however, there is a pleasant square that is enjoyed by many in summer (above), and the water-jet fountains are a great draw for children. St Andrew's church was demolished in 1947 but the spire was left intact. Known locally as the Glovers' Needle because of its local connection with the erstwhile glove-making industry, it is a centre of attention to spotters of peregrine falcons.

THE FARRIERS ARMS, FISH STREET

THREE LITTLE GIRLS play outside the Farriers Arms in Fish Street in the old photograph on the left, unconcerned about traffic or any other dangers of modern life. Perhaps a more innocent age, but an unlikely scene now since Fish Street and its surrounds are no longer residential. The photograph was taken in 1960, before the housing clearances and the development of Deansway (quite close to this location) as a busy through traffic route.

THE VIEW IS little changed today, and Fish Street is an attractive, if slightly hidden, area with an historical feel, although the street now serves a different purpose (above). It is used mainly as one of the walking routes between High Street and Copenhagen Street's popular car park, or for access to its two pubs, the church and a few shops.

MEALCHEAPEN STREET

THE OLD PHOTOGRAPH looks west up Mealcheapen Street, towards St Swithin's church. It was taken sometime before 1967, and the sign for the Reindeer public house can be seen on the left. It had competitors in the inn directly opposite and the Royal Exchange on the corner of Cornmarket.

THE ROYAL EXCHANGE has survived as the Exchange, a busy pub often showing live sports. It is, however, the only watering hole left in the street: the Reindeer's neighbour is now a shop, and a similar fate has befallen the Reindeer itself. The Reindeer's name lives on in the Reindeer Court shopping centre, a tasteful collection of individual enterprises and route through to the Shambles.

THE CORNER OF
TRINITY STREET AND
MEALCHEAPEN STREET

E.M. PARSONS LOOKS like it has finished its sale and closed, the sign over the shopfront having disappeared and looking very empty (left). This is Mealcheapen Street going off to the right, with the photographer's back to St Swithin's church. Trinity Street is the road going to the left. The ladies at the barrow seem to be doing a good trade in this mid-1930s shot, and there may well have been a flower seller in front of the church.

THE CORNER AND the yards beyond have been replaced in recent times by this post-modern building society structure that echoes the Dutch gables of its neighbours (above). The appropriately named Holland and Barrett has superseded the shop selling Finest Colonial Meats.

REINDEER INN/
REINDEER COURT

THE COURTYARD OF the Reindeer Inn, possibly from the 1920s, can be seen in the old photograph on the left. The sun is filtering through the glass roof and a precariously-placed baby is being juddered over the cobbles as flowers are being delivered. The Reindeer was, of course, one of Worcester's old staging inns and this would have been the way through to the stable block.

THE INN IS no more, but Reindeer Court remains a pleasingly successful conversion of the old buildings into a shopping court with cafés and a restaurant. It still has its original cobbled floor, and the clatter of hooves and carriage wheels can be easily imagined.

PUMP STREET

PUMP STREET LEAVES the High Street opposite Copenhagen Street and runs down to New Street (opposite). Now a pedestrian precinct, it has a few old buildings and some rather unattractive new ones. The interesting part of this photograph (right), taken in 1965, is the gabled timber-framed shops at the centre, one of which has been rendered and painted. At one time this double-fronted building was the Horse and Jockey Inn, whose records date back to 1766, although it was possibly much older. On the extreme left of the view is the Eagle Vaults bar at the start of Friar Street – the Horse and Jockey's former next-door neighbour. Further up towards High Street was the Swan, housed in a similar timber-framed building. The

Famous Army Stores has optimistically taken a short lease on the nearest half of the former Horse and Jockey and 'will open shortly'.

BEYOND THE EAGLE Vaults none of the old buildings remain, and their replacements are a non-cohesive collection (left). The High Street at the top throngs busily, and the crowds flow down Pump Street towards the Shambles on the right of the photograph, Friar Street to the left.

THE CATHEDRAL FROM ACROSS THE RIVER

THE CATHEDRAL IS Worcester's defining visual feature. The city exists in its present form because of the cathedral, which has always exerted a visual pull to those with artistic tendencies. Its location next to the river has preserved its open views and gives the impression, even today, of a much more rural location. The scene to the left was recorded on Easter Monday in 1952.

THE SCENE TODAY is a familiar one, even though the well-trodden riverside walk has received a coat of tarmac. Sketchers working here nowadays would see a much more fractured view of the cathedral as tree growth has emerged. The rural peace of the area, however, is not much changed.

THE WATER GATE

AT THE WEST side of the cathedral there are the ruins of its previous incarnation, the monastery. This early photograph (left) shows the Water Gate, the only surviving medieval city gate. On the lower part of the gate, leading from the river, are recorded the various flood levels over the years. St Andrew's church tower can be seen in the background, in those days it was attached to a church, but competing with the now extinct factory chimneys.

THESE DAYS, THE route down from the cathedral to the river is mostly unchanged, and the walkway offers a good viewing position for the frequent rowing teams speeding by. The Water Gate's records now show the most recent major floods of November 2000 and July 2007, the latter getting close to the highest recorded water levels. With the changes to the Copenhagen Street area, the more distant view has changed considerably, illustrating the changes to Worcester's industry.

THE CATHEDRAL AND FERRY

A LONG-ESTABLISHED FERRY service took passengers the short distance across the river until it was closed shortly after the Second World War. It ran to and from the Water Gate, seen here on the right of the picture on the left, with its steps leading to the water. The west bank here provides opportunities for fairly complete views of the cathedral and its environs.

RATHER MORE OBSCURED by trees, it is difficult to find an entire view of the cathedral from the current leafy walks on this side of the river (above). The usefulness of the ferry is understandable to anyone who makes the journey to this point from the cathedral; the route via the bridge is a time-consuming, if pleasant, one. Fortunately, the ferry has returned in recent years, operating in the summer months as a money-raising charity enterprise.

VIEW FROM THE
CATHEDRAL TOWER

THE CENTRE OF the view opposite, taken from the cathedral tower, shows St Michael's church in 1954, with the Punch Bowl Inn to the right. The road in the foreground is College Street, and behind St Michael's is a rare view of the now extinct Lich Street. Friar Street and its continuation, New Street, can just be discerned running from top left, past the timber-framed buildings. The entrance to High Street is just outside the picture at the left-hand end of Lich Street, and no doubt that is where the bus is heading.

ST MICHAEL'S, THE Punch Bowl Inn, Lich Street and all immediately beyond have now gone, and the vast featureless roofscapes of the car park, hotel and shopping centre offer little in terms of a modern aesthetic aerial view (above). The redevelopment began in the mid 1960s, with the Lychgate Centre (now Cathedral Plaza) opening in 1968. St Michael's churchyard and the top part of Lich Street have made way for the roundabout, part of the revised traffic flow scheme. Elgar's statue now marks the end of the High Street.

COLLEGE YARD

THIS VIEW HAS changed very little in over fifty
years. College Yard is the curved road that runs from
College Street (by the roundabout at the cathedral
end of the High Street) round to the cathedral
door. Taken in the summer of 1953, the bunting is
probably for the coronation. The shop is catering for
the visitor, selling postcards, souvenirs and porcelain
produced by the Royal Worcester factory, which is
just a short walk away.

THE HOUSES HAVE been cleared of their ivy,
iron posts now deter car parking and Bygones
of Worcester now sell antiques from the shop.

The Victorian postbox has probably been relocated from a more obscure position, and Royal Worcester – to the regret of many people – is no longer a presence in the city. Its factory area has now been redeveloped as upmarket flats.

COLLEGE STREET FROM THE CATHEDRAL

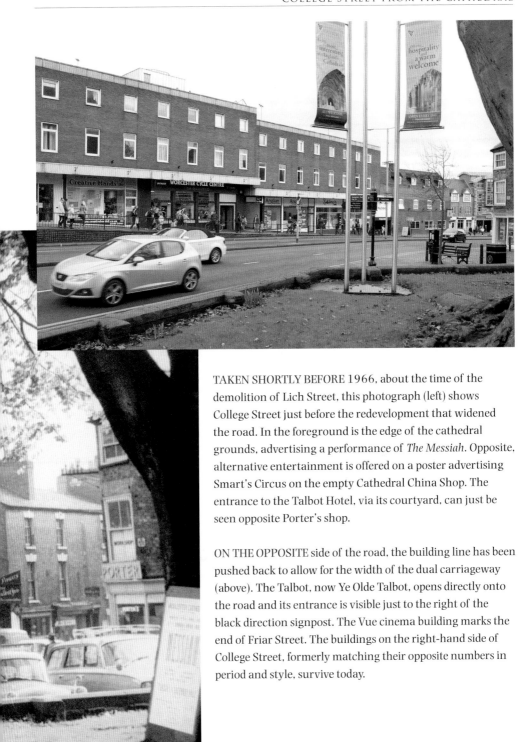

TAKEN SHORTLY BEFORE 1966, about the time of the demolition of Lich Street, this photograph (left) shows College Street just before the redevelopment that widened the road. In the foreground is the edge of the cathedral grounds, advertising a performance of *The Messiah*. Opposite, alternative entertainment is offered on a poster advertising Smart's Circus on the empty Cathedral China Shop. The entrance to the Talbot Hotel, via its courtyard, can just be seen opposite Porter's shop.

ON THE OPPOSITE side of the road, the building line has been pushed back to allow for the width of the dual carriageway (above). The Talbot, now Ye Olde Talbot, opens directly onto the road and its entrance is visible just to the right of the black direction signpost. The Vue cinema building marks the end of Friar Street. The buildings on the right-hand side of College Street, formerly matching their opposite numbers in period and style, survive today.

COLLEGE STREET LOOKING SOUTH

A VIEW SOUTH down College Street taken in 1961 before the cloud of demolition hung heavily over it (left). The Talbot's courtyard entrance is announced on the east side of the street. The entrance to Edgar Street is on the west side, after the large building in the centre, and the 'No Left Turn' sign refers to Friar Street. The main route south out of Worcester in the age before the M5 gives an impression of a gentler age.

THE ROAD WAS widened in 1966 and the buildings on the left are of that time (above). The Talbot now straddles the corner of College Street and Friar Street, which no longer has a left turn ban. The view into the pub's entrance, seen here far left, gives an insight into its former structure.

SIDBURY
LOOKING NORTH

SIDBURY (MEANING 'SOUTH of the borough') is the southerly
continuation of College Street after the junction with the City Walls
Road. In 1898, coming into the city from the south, Sidbury curved
round to the right to become Friar Street, with College Street on a
left fork just before. A weary traveller could find refreshment in the
café on the left of the right-hand photograph or the Red Lion Inn
opposite. The focal point in this picturesque village-like view is the
cathedral, but the timber-framed building just before the road bends
to the right is the Commandery, which was then in private hands.

THE RED LION Inn is now a Thai restaurant but the structure of the road on that side is largely
unchanged (left). All the buildings on the left side of the road, however, up to the junction
with Edgar Street, are now gone. Widening of the road and of the canal bridge caused major
remodelling in the late 1950s, allowing the canal and its attractive locks and walkways to be
exposed to public view. The present bridge wall commemorates Sidbury Gate, an entrance to the
city stormed by Parliamentary troops during the English Civil War. The last battle of the war took
place in Worcester on 3 November 1651.

THE COMMANDERY

A CLOSE UP of the Commandery frontage. The main parts of the building, in an H-shaped formation, are behind this and have undergone many changes since it was created in the fifteenth century as St Wulstan's Hospital, attached to a church. At the time of the old photograph (right), in 1908, the whole building was owned by Littlebury's printers, who leased the front to shops.

THE COMMANDERY HAS changed and developed over the years, and was extensively refurbished in the mid 2000s . These days, the Commandery is a busy museum and a venue for events as diverse as re-enactments of various periods, early music events and open-air theatre.

RIVERSIDE, RIVER TRIP

ONE OF WORCESTER'S river trip boats, looking oversubscribed, can be seen in the old photograph on the left. It is 1912 and Worcester's famous swans are in evidence. The opening just slightly left of the centre of the picture was Hood Street. Copenhagen Street runs up alongside the last of the central factory blocks, and two children are walking away from what is now the area of the fountains. The riverside area was then a very busy mix of industry, housing and pleasure seekers.

THE MODERN LINES of Worcester College of Technology's buildings now dominate the area behind the quay, whose shoreline elevation has changed in line with the newer bridge (above). The three large buildings to the right of the older picture and below the spire remain. The Gascoine Kent warehouse – traces of the external signwriting can still be seen on its wall – and those to the right have different uses today, being, respectively, an apartment building, a restaurant and a café/restaurant.

RIVERSIDE, SOUTH PARADE

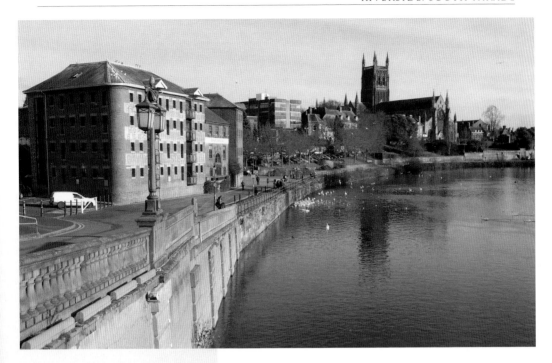

AFTER COPENHAGEN STREET, South Parade becomes South Quay. In this 1892 view (left), probably taken from the bridge, the bright weather has got a lot of people out for their perambulations. If this was a Sunday, the group of children at the bottom of Copenhagen Street may well have just come out of the Sunday school.

COPENHAGEN STREET IS still there, though of course much altered. Other parts of the area have disappeared over the last hundred years. Still dominating, and now not in competition with the tall chimneys, Worcester Cathedral provides the focal point for river views. Worcester no longer trades by the river, but the quayside is still a place for ramblings.

THE RIVER
AND
CATHEDRAL

PHOTOGRAPHED IN 1892, the Severn's sweep around the bend gives a view of both banks. On the west (right-hand) bank, a group of young men in straw boaters is inspecting the shoreline, a mother is attending to a child, and several people are lying on the grass enjoying the sun or the view. The opposite bank has its usual complement of strollers, some with parasols.

THERE IS A rather less involving view now with a car park and the college buildings taking centre stage (left). There is, however, a better view of the old palace, and newer tree growth is starting to hide the more recent structures. The west bank, still a place for a quiet stroll, is also more tree-lined, yet seeming more cared-for.

NORTH PARADE

A BUSY DAY on North Parade (left), looking north from the bridge in 1899. People are going about their business, carters are doing their deliveries and even a flock of sheep is being driven along, reminding us of Worcester's very close rural surrounds. The timbered inn is the Old Rectifying House, whose name refers to the spirit rectification that happened at the back of it. The main part of the distillery was on the opposite bank, presumably necessitating frequent traffic of barrels across the river. The bridge dates from 1781, and replaced one from medieval times. This photograph shows the road rising to meet the bridge and the pedestrian route staying level to a small tunnel. This lower path was also followed by the little rail track for boat loading equipment.

THE LATER BRIDGE dates from 1932 and has a wider access road whose gradient has been reduced by raising the level of the road (above). There is now no pedestrian tunnel, and the Old Rectifying House's ground floor windows are now very close to the ground. The housing at the centre of the older photograph, including T. Wintle's business, has given way to part of a one-way traffic circulation system and car park.

THE SHAMBLES, ST SWITHIN'S

THE SHAMBLES IS, traditionally, a street of butcher's shops and Worcester's Shambles had many listed in Victorian times. There are two memorable buildings in this picture on the left: St Swithin's church and the black-and-white premises of J. and F. Hall, an ironmonger and general store. This view is from the early 1960s and shows a busy shopping day, possibly a Saturday.

HALL'S PREMISES WERE gone by 1962. Even though a campaign to save the building was under way in Worcester, the plans were overruled by Whitehall's central government. After a brief spell of an unhindered view of St Swithin's church, it was replaced by the current building – not the most sympathetic to its surroundings. The church is further obscured nowadays by a couple of fast food stands.

THE SHAMBLES LOOKING
TO ST SWITHIN'S STREET

THIS IS HOW the Shambles looked before 1962 (left). J. and F. Hall's timbered premises can just be seen jutting out into the street at the end of the left-hand line of shops, but the removal of old property has already started. The street illuminations and damp weather suggest that this may be a post-Christmas view. The shops of St Swithin's Street can be seen at the end.

THE ONLY SURVIVOR of the west side of the street is the former H.D. Andrews shop – half of the three-gabled building on the left in the previous photograph. A slightly jarring mix of variously positioned cuboids overpowers this little building and contrasts sharply with the more even line of Georgian structures on the opposite side (above). Reindeer Court has an entrance here and its traders have positioned their advertising to attract shoppers.

QUEEN STREET

QUEEN STREET RUNS parallel to Trinity
Street, and this is a view from its St Nicholas
Street end which was in the process of
demolition when the photograph on the left
was taken in July 1966. The building on
the right is the old Worcester Co-operative
building. The most distant building is
Cornmarket's Public Hall.

THE CO-OPERATIVE STORE has since been
replaced with a much less interesting looking
structure, and all the buildings on the left are
gone (above). Queen Street's only traffic use
now is as the entrance to the Cornmarket car
park, a space for which all these buildings
were sacrificed. Beyond this, the City Walls
Road and the Lowesmoor area, here being
redeveloped, make up the view.

CORNMARKET AT NEW STREET CORNER

THE CORNMARKET IS the space between the Public Hall on the right; Mealcheapen Street running into the distance, after the Royal Exchange Inn (now the Exchange); and New Street on the left. The market was one of Worcester's medieval marketplaces, and the Public Hall was a concert venue used for, among other things, the Three Choirs Festival during Worcester's turn to host. The old photograph on the left was taken in a chilly-looking February in 1966.

CORNMARKET NOWADAYS REFERS to the whole area including, of course, the car park that has replaced most of the space to the right of the 1966 photograph. The Public Hall did not survive the year, but the rest of the area is still an attractive reminder of Worcester's past (above).

CORNMARKET LOOKING TOWARDS LOWESMOOR

LOOKING EAST FROM the Cornmarket in the direction of this (possibly Edwardian) photograph
(left), St Martin's Gate was the road to the right, between the shops in the middle distance
and the Plough Inn, which can be seen on the far left. St Martin's Gate marked one of
several medieval entrances to the city and led to St Martin's church, which was behind the
photographer and slightly to his or her left. Turning right, in front of L.F. Batten you would be
facing King Charles' House and the entrance to New Street.

L.F. BATTEN'S BUILDING has been carved off its next-door neighbour (with the pentagonal
window pediments) and has disappeared along with the shops behind it and the Plough Inn. The
Cornmarket and Lowesmoor areas, formerly a cosy walk past the Plough via Silver Street, have
been split by the City Walls Road dual carriageway, and St Martin's Gate now only exists as a road
name on the east side, starting from a roundabout just behind the buildings in the foreground.
The Plough Inn itself would have occupied the area a little to the left of the bedroom furniture
store and slightly towards the camera.

KING CHARLES' HOUSE

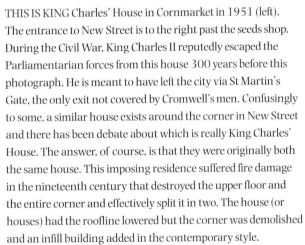

THIS IS KING Charles' House in Cornmarket in 1951 (left). The entrance to New Street is to the right past the seeds shop. During the Civil War, King Charles II reputedly escaped the Parliamentarian forces from this house 300 years before this photograph. He is meant to have left the city via St Martin's Gate, the only exit not covered by Cromwell's men. Confusingly to some, a similar house exists around the corner in New Street and there has been debate about which is really King Charles' House. The answer, of course, is that they were originally both the same house. This imposing residence suffered fire damage in the nineteenth century that destroyed the upper floor and the entire corner and effectively split it in two. The house (or houses) had the roofline lowered but the corner was demolished and an infill building added in the contemporary style.

TODAY, KING CHARLES' House in Cornmarket is two shops and its namesake in New Street is a restaurant, while the 'new' corner is a separate unit housing a hairdresser (above). Prior to the fire, the house was an imposing three-storey building with nine gables and presumably many spaces for hiding a king on the run.

SHRUB HILL ROAD

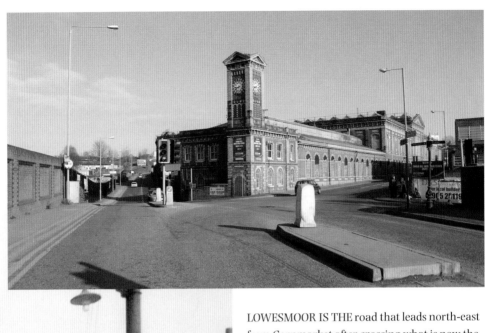

LOWESMOOR IS THE road that leads north-east from Cornmarket after crossing what is now the City Walls Road. It has been an area of industry and poverty, much like the riverside section of the city. Continuing away from the city centre, it divides into Lowesmoor Terrace and Lowesmoor Place, the former leading into Rainbow Hill and the latter leading to this view (left), with another fork (the left goes to the gas works and the other, to the right, is Shrub Hill Road, leading to the railway station). Dominating the junction is the Heenan and Froude factory, an impressive Italianate Victorian landmark.

LOOKING AT THE same scene now (above), the gantry on the left has gone and the road to the left is now Tolladine Road, a major route. Heenan and Froude's building has lost its little front garden and is now split into industrial units.

SHRUB HILL ROAD,
HEENAN AND FROUDE

THIS IS THE Heenan and Froude building seen from Shrub Hill Road in the 1950s (left). Its clock is clearly visible even at this end, and its cream and red brickwork gives it a unique look. It was not always the factory of Heenan and Froude. It started life as the engineering works for the railway station and changed hands several times. It was, fortunately, empty at the time of the Worcester Exhibition in 1882 and proved an ideal location for it. Next door to the building, on the right in the picture, was Holy Trinity church, its entrance shrouded by foliage.

THERE IS LITTLE change to the view now (above), except that Holy Trinity church is gone, demolished in the late 1960s. Its roof, formerly that of the cathedral's Guesten Hall, lives on at the Avoncroft Museum of Historic Buildings in Bromsgrove. The steps, formerly leading to the church from its gatepost, remain.

NORTHWALL HOUSE

NORTHWALL HOUSE (LEFT) was part of Worcester Grammar School for Girls. It had its entrance in The Butts, opposite the Paul Pry pub, and was separated from the road by its gardens, which must have given it a certain tranquillity despite its city centre location.

FORTUNATELY, THE BUILDING survives today, though the same view of it is not possible now, its gardens having been replaced by brick block industrial units servicing the motor trade. Planning approval for this must have raised some uncomfortable questions. After a period of dereliction, Northwall House is now in private hands and is run as offices.

ALBERT SIMONS' SHOP

ALBERT SIMONS HAD this shop (left) at the corner of Sansome Walk and Wood Terrace. Here he poses happily with his family, cat and a well turned out shop display. Just to the right, across Wood Terrace, was St Mary's church, and this locality would no doubt have ensured the thriving business he clearly had.

THE DAYS OF the corner shop were mostly over by the end of the 1960s when supermarkets and mass personal transportation brought a different form of convenience. Selling most daily living requirements, these small shops offered local supplies during the day, food and drink for the evening that could be purchased on the way home, and an Aladdin's cave of delights for children. The business of both this shop and the church is now no more; Albert Simons' door and windows have been bricked up, and the church is now St Mary's Court, a conversion to flats.

NASH'S HOUSE

IN NEW STREET, which leads from Cornmarket through to its continuation, Friar Street, Nash's House stands out as a fine example of the wood builder's craft. A four-storey jettied house, it was owned by John Nash, alderman, mayor and Member of Parliament, whose family made their fortune in clothing. By the time of the old photograph (left), in 1905, it housed a picture frame manufacturer. Looking at this photograph, the popularity of galoshes can be understood. Much trailing of mud must have happened in an afternoon's shopping.

NEW STREET IS little changed in terms of its structure, although Nash's next-door neighbour has had its roofline lowered a little and has undergone a change of use. Nash's House now incorporates a ground floor café and the mud has long gone from the street outside.

Other titles published by The History Press

Haunted Worcestershire
ANTHONY POULTON-SMITH

Anthony Poulton-Smith takes the reader on a fascinating A-Z tour of the haunted hotspots of Worcestershire, telling strange tales of spectral sightings, active poltergeists and restless spirits appearing in streets, inns, churches, estates, public buildings and private homes across the area. *Haunted Worcestershire* includes tales from Worcester, Bewdley, Droitwich, Bromsgrove, Tenbury Wells and Stourport-on-Severn and is sure to appeal to all those intrigued by Worcestershire's haunted heritage.

978 0 7524 4872 5

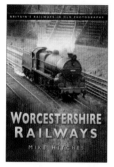

Worcestershire Railways
MIKE HITCHES

The railways which operated in Worcestershire were controlled by the Midland Railway and the Great Western Railway, whose struggle for supremacy had considerable effect on the development of railways in the county. The photographs in this book illustrate not only the county's trains and locomotives but also many of the stations, locosheds and locomotive building works, and the picture is completed with timetables and shed allocation.

978 0 7524 5057 5

Worcestershire: Family History Guidebook
VANESSA MORGAN

In *Worcestershire: Family History Guidebook*, professional local genealogist Vanessa Morgan takes us on a fascinating and easy-to-follow journey from deciding to research your Worcestershire ancestors right through to discovering more about how they lived and worked. Family history isn't just about names and dates; this book will help you to put the flesh on bones.

978 0 7524 5969 1

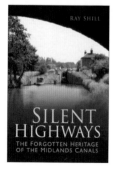

Silent Highways: The Forgotten Heritage of the Midlands Canals
RAY SHILL

This fascinating book delves into the forgotten history of the Midland and border canal infrastructure, including the Grand Union, Staffordshire & Worcestershire, Stourbridge, Stratford, Trent & Mersey, Worcester & Birmingham canals amongst others. *Silent Highways* also recognises the skills of the engineers who designed and built the canals and had such an influence on the waterways in this region despite the hardships of working conditions and poor finance. A must for all local and canal historians.

978 0 7524 5842 7

Visit our website and discover thousands of other History Press books.
www.thehistorypress.co.uk